Table of Contents

Teaching Guide

Introduction

This book is one of six in a series designed to encourage the reading enjoyment of young students. Subject matter was carefully chosen to correspond to student interests. Skills were selected to reinforce understanding of the readings and to promote confidence in independent reading.

Content

The contents of each book have been drawn from seven specific categories: 1) biography, 2) amazing facts, 3) mystery and intrigue, 4) sports stars and events, 5) visual and performing arts, 6) wonders in science and nature, and 7) excerpts from mythology and literature.

The popular biographies, sports figures, and artists give students an opportunity to identify with people who are familiar to them. Those figures who are unknown to the students' experience give them clues to the wide diversity of current society in many countries. A look behind the scenes of a famous life holds a never-ending fascination.

In addition to spy stories and tales of ghostly encounters, the mystery selections often offer a puzzling situation to solve or the beginning of a story which must be completed by the reader.

Science and nature selections are chosen to generate interest in new and untapped areas of the readers' knowledge and to encourage them to explore further.

Samples of a wide variety of stories from mythology and literature have been included. It is hoped that this brief encounter with some of the great story lines will motivate the student to seek out and read the entire selection.

Skills

The skills employed in this series are drawn from traditional educational objectives. The five comprehension areas practiced in this series are: main idea, recognition of significant details, use of context clues for determining word meaning, inference, and drawing conclusions. All categories are not necessarily represented at the conclusion of each story. Questioning format varies from book to book to avoid predictability. Where space permits, a follow-through activity has been included. These are expected to lead to self-motivated reading or to valuable discussion. The activity also gives the teacher an opportunity to award extra credit.

Upon completion of each collection of stories and accompanying skill activities, students should show improvement in the areas practiced; i.e., the ability to locate, evaluate, and predict, as well as to conduct study and research.

Readability

The reading level of each book is essentially two years below the interest level. Readability levels were confirmed by the Spache formula for the lower grades and the Dale-Chall formula for the upper grades. Each book is suitable for a variety of students working at a range of reading levels. The lower readability allows older students with reading deficiencies to enjoy high-interest content with minimum frustration. The comprehension activities provide a growth opportunity for capable students as well. The high-interest content should help to motivate students at any level.

The teacher should keep in mind that supplying easy-to-read content provides a good setting for learning new skills. Thus, comprehension development can best take place where vocabulary and sentence constraints ensure student understanding. It should be obvious that the concept of main idea, as well as the nature of an inference, can be seen best where the total content of a selection is well within a reader's grasp.

Finally, the material is dedicated to the principle that the more a student reads, the better he or she reads, and the greater is the appreciation of the printed word.

Answer Key

Page 1
1. c
2. b
3. b
4. c
5. Answers will vary.

Page 2
1. c
2. b
3. a
4. b
5. Answers will vary.
6. Answers will vary.

Page 4
1. c
2. b
3. b
4. a
5. c

Page 5
1. b
2. a
3. a
4. c
5. b

Page 6
1. b
2. a
3. b
4. a

Page 8
1. b
2. a
3. c
4. Answers will vary.
5. Answers will vary.

Page 9
1. c
2. a
3. b
4. a
5. b

Page 12
1. c
2. b
3. a
4. b
5. a

Page 13
1. c
2. a
3. b
4. a
5. c
6. b

Page 14
1. c
2. a
3. c
4. b
5. b

Page 15
1. c
2. a
3. b
4. non-fiction
5. b

Page 17
1. c
2. a
3. a
4. c
5. b
6. b

Page 19
1. b
2. c
3. a
4. Answers will vary.
5. Answers will vary.

Page 21
1. b
2. a
3. c
4. Answers will vary.
5. a

Page 23
1. rafting
2. b
3. c
4. b
5. Answers will vary.

Page 25
1. a
2. c
3. b
4. Answers will vary.
5. a

Page 27
1. b
2. a
3. a
4. a
5. b

Page 29
1. c
2. b
3. b
4. a
5. a

MP3391

Page 31
1. b
2. a
3. c
4. a
5. a
6. b
7. b
8. c
9. c

Page 32
1. b
2. c
3. a
4. c
5. a

Page 34
1. b
2. c
3. c
4. b
5. a

Page 35
1. c
2. a
3. c
4. c
5. a
6. b
7. b

Page 36
1. c
2. a
3. a
4. b
5. b
6. a

Page 37
1. b
2. c
3. a
4. c
5. b
6. b

Page 38
1. b
2. a
3. c
4. c
5. c
6. b
7. c

Page 40
1. b
2. c
3. a
4. b
5. c
6. a
7. b
8. c
9. b

Page 41
1. b
2. b
3. b
4. c
5. a
6. b

Page 42
1. c
2. a
3. b
4. b
5. b
6. b
7. c

Page 44
1. b
2. c
3. b
4. a
5. c
6. b
7. b
8. a

HyperSoar Jets

How would you like to fly anywhere in the world in only two hours? It may be possible in a few years. Aerospace engineers at the United States Department of Energy are working on a new aircraft. It is called the HyperSoar jet and it will fly at 6700 miles per hour. Most car drivers can get a speeding ticket for traveling over 60 miles per hour. Imagine moving over 6000 miles per hour! The HyperSoar jet would travel at Mach 10. This is ten times faster than the speed of sound.

Most planes would burn up if they traveled that fast through the atmosphere. Heat would build up outside the plane and the engine would melt. But the HyperSoar designers took care of that problem. The jet will fly outside the Earth's atmosphere where the temperature is cooler. The jet will skip down into Earth's atmosphere every two minutes, just long enough for the air to ignite the jet's engine and send it back into space. The jet will then turn off its engine and coast back down to the Earth's atmosphere for another boost into space. The effect has been described somewhat like skipping stones across the water. When a stone hits the surface of the water, it is bounced back into the air until it comes down and skips across the water again. It would take only about twenty-five "skips" for the jet to fly from the United States to Japan.

The jet would soar up and down between 110,000 to 200,000 feet. It would be a little like riding a roller coaster. But passengers could be in for more fun. As the jet soars past 130,000 feet, it leaves Earth's gravitational pull. This means that passengers could experience weightlessness. If they took off their seatbelts, they could float around inside the plane.

As much fun as the jet ride sounds, it is still a long way from takeoff. The engines are still being developed. The cost of the jets would be very expensive. But its developers say that the HyperSoar would hold 500 passengers. With this many people buying flight tickets, the cost can be kept down. If all plans go well, someday you may be able to fly around the world and still be home in time for dinner.

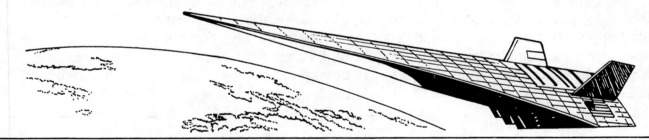

Main Idea
1. People would want to fly on this jet because
   a. the cost would be kept down.
   b. it would be more fun than a carnival ride.
   c. you could reach your destination very quickly.

Significant Details
2. The Earth loses its gravitational pull above
   a. 200,000 feet.
   b. 130,000 feet.
   c. 110,000 feet.
3. Mach 10 is
   a. a car.
   b. a speed.
   c. a jet.

Inference
4. How does the HyperSoar take advantage of natural conditions?
   a. It travels faster than the speed of sound.
   b. It skims across the water to get momentum.
   c. It uses Earth's atmosphere to start its engines.

Drawing Conclusions
5. What are some possible uses of the HyperSoar jet?

   _____

   _____

   _____

   _____

Special Olympics

Training for the Olympics takes every bit of strength and determination a competitor can gather. Many people have strength and determination, but because they have a developmental disability, are not able to participate in the regular Olympics.

In 1968, the Special Olympics for the developmentally disabled was started, and a whole wonderful world was opened to over a million people. Contestants could participate in many events from swimming to racing. The events are now run on local, national, and international levels. Eunice Kennedy Shriver, sister of the late President John F. Kennedy, began a special athletic camp for children with developmental disabilities right in her own backyard. Using money from the Joseph P. Kennedy Foundation, the special camp moved from Eunice's backyard to local camps and schools across the country.

Interest spread from the United States to 35 foreign countries. Now competitions are held internationally. They follow the same form as the regular Olympic games, specializing in both summer and winter events. Competitors come from all over the world. Children and adults are of many ages and have many different levels of ability. Many of those taking part may need help remembering the rules of the game or competition. But no matter what their level of ability, these athletes are all there for the challenge and to do their very best.

Privately-funded programs provide coaches, trainers, and special equipment for Special Olympics. Coaches and trainers receive special instruction on coaching and working with athletes with special needs. These special athletes have to train very hard to participate in their events. They often have to train harder than a regular athlete because they may have many unusual obstacles to overcome. Coaches and trainers work with the athletes all year. Skill and confidence levels are increased and soon athletes are ready for competition.

Thousands of volunteers are ready, too. Volunteers are at the Olympics to organize teams, line up athletes, and time the events. One of the most important volunteer jobs is that of a "hugger." Each participant that crosses the finish line receives a hug of congratulations from a Special Olympics volunteer. These hugs can be better rewards than money, scholarships, or other prizes. The athletes know that someone else cares about their achievement.

These athletes compete for the sheer joy of the accomplishment. They know they have beaten the odds and have done their personal best.

Main Idea
1. Special Olympics are held for
   a. skiers.
   b. foreign athletes.
   c. developmentally disabled athletes.

Significant Details
2. The Special Olympics is partly financed by
   a. the Rhodes scholarship fund.
   b. the Joseph P. Kennedy Foundation.
   c. foreign countries.

Context Clues
3. An *obstacle* is
   a. anything that gets in the way and blocks progress.
   b. a prize.
   c. a foundation.

4. A *competitor* is
   a. a hugger.
   b. one who takes part in a contest.
   c. a coach.

Drawing Conclusions
5. List at least three different feelings or emotions you might experience if you competed in an event in the Olympics.

   _____

   _____

   _____

Following Through
6. Read about special athletes. Find out how their disabilities interfere with their sports, and what methods they use to overcome these disabilities.

The Way to Johnson City

Brian sat back in the seat and looked out the window. It seemed strange that although he was fifteen, he had never ridden a train before. He had traveled by air with his parents and visited his grandparents by bus, but this was his first train ride. He stretched his legs and relaxed. The door at the front of the car opened and Brian saw a conductor come through. The conductor stopped at each seat to check tickets. Brian got out his ticket and was ready when the conductor got to him.

"Your destination, sir?" asked the conductor.

"Johnson City," said Brian. "I'm going to visit a friend."

The conductor looked surprised. "There is no such stop on this run," he said.

"But here is my ticket," said Brian. "The man in the ticket office sold it to me and said it would get me to Johnson City."

"Sorry," said the conductor. "I never heard of Johnson City and I've been on this run for fourteen years."

Finish the story. If necessary, continue on another paper.

_____

_____

_____

_____

_____

_____

_____

_____

_____

_____

_____

_____

_____

Ken Griffey, Jr.

Ken Griffey, Jr. has been called one of the greatest baseball players of the 1990s. In his first at bat in the major leagues, he hit a double. A week later in front of a hometown crowd, he hit his first major league home run. He has continued to hit extra base hits throughout his career.

The Seattle Mariners of the American League chose Griffey as their first-round pick in the 1987 draft. He made the team in 1989 at age 19 and had a fine rookie season. He tied a club record with hits in eight games in a row and set a new team record by reaching base safely 11 straight times. Griffey also displayed talent as a center fielder. He led all league outfielders with six double plays his rookie year.

It is not surprising that Griffey became a baseball player. His father, Ken Griffey, Sr. played 19 years in the major leagues. He played in three All-Star games and helped the National League's Cincinnati Reds win two world championships. Ken, Jr. watched his dad play for years and talked to him about every game.

The elder Griffey taught his son the importance of consistency in catching, throwing, and hitting. The two of them practiced these skills over and over. Ken, Jr. used what he learned from his father to become an excellent outfielder and an aggressive baserunner, as well as an outstanding hitter.

When Ken, Jr. joined the Mariners, the Griffeys became the first father and son ever to play in the major leagues at the same time. Ken, Sr. became a Mariner in 1990. On September 14, when they both appeared in the line-up, in the first inning, they hit the only back-to-back, father-and-son home runs in baseball history.

Ken Griffey, Sr. retired from baseball in 1991, but his son remained as valuable as any player in baseball. He has been named to every American League All-Star team since 1990. He has received the Silver Slugger Award six times. This award is given to those batters who have hit the most extra-base hits.

He has earned the Gold Glove Award every year since 1990, an American League record for outfielders. In 1993 Griffey set a league record for outfielders after 542 fielding changes in a row without an error. Seattle and baseball fans everywhere will not soon forget Ken Griffey, Jr.

Main Idea

1. Ken Griffey, Jr. is well-known in baseball because
   a. his father was a major-league player.
   b. he plays on a championship team.
   c. he has set many records and won many awards.

Significant Details

2. The Seattle Mariners play in the
   a. World Series.
   b. American League.
   c. All-Star games.
3. Ken Griffey, Jr. has set
   a. base-stealing records.
   b. hitting and fielding records.
   c. pitching records.

Inference

4. Ken Griffey, Jr. must admire his dad because
   a. he followed his father's example and took his advice.
   b. Ken, Sr. is a well-known baseball coach.
   c. his father had earned a lot of money.

Drawing Conclusions

5. If Ken Griffey, Jr. continues to play baseball in the year 2000 and beyond, he will probably
   a. get tired of the sport.
   b. try to become a pitcher.
   c. set more records and win more awards.

Bananas of the Future

If you hear of someone serving kiwi fruit or papayas for breakfast, you might think they were ordered from the South Sea Islands. Not so. At produce counters in grocery stores in the middle of the U.S., you could find these and other even more unusual fruits for sale. Customers are suddenly flooding the stores with requests and making extra trips to find new and interesting produce.

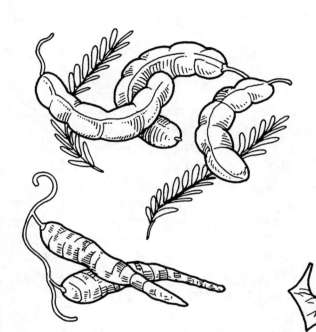

The head of the country's largest chain of markets sees a big change almost overnight in what Americans are seeking. Apples, oranges, peaches, and grapefruit are still favorites. But more and more, people are eager to add some adventure to their diet. Now these interesting fruits and vegetables are available. Most have been introduced to the country by immigrants. Large numbers of immigrants live near Florida and California. These states are the two main bases for the new industry.

Some of the things to add to a shopping list are tamarinds, lady apples, oyster plants, delantri, jicama, or fiddle-head greens. Growing these is an everyday chore for some Filipinos, Cubans, and Mexicans. U.S. growers are even pulling up their grapefruit trees to replace them with these new fruits. One man now has a grove of small, thin-skinned red bananas instead of grapefruit. A red banana? That's only the beginning. Try a black radish, a curly string bean, a star apple. . . .

Main Idea
1. America's food market has seen an increase in
    a. diet foods.
    b. unusual and exotic fruits.
    c. apples, oranges, and grapefruit.

Significant Details
2. The main bases for the country's new produce industry are
    a. Florida and California.
    b. Philippines, Cuba, and Mexico.
    c. South Sea Islands.

Context Clues
3. Customers are buying unusual *produce*.
    a. fruits and vegetables
    b. special foods for people on a diet
    c. products in a store

Inference
4. People in different countries
    a. eat the same foods.
    b. speak the same language.
    c. prepare different dishes.

Drawing Conclusions
5. Delantri, jicama, and fiddle-head greens are
    a. Mexican coins.
    b. new produce brought by immigrants.
    c. Cuban farm workers.

Following Through
6. Design your own backyard garden. Decide which crops you would like to raise. Make a list of the care and feeding of your crops.

MP3391

Will Smith

When an elementary school teacher in Philadelphia nicknamed one of her young students, "The Prince," she had no way of knowing how famous that nickname would become. Young Will Smith had such a smooth way of talking, his teachers said he sounded as if he were born of royalty. Will was always polite and had a way of being friendly with everyone. His easy-going manner and sense of humor made him well-liked by his classmates.

Will had always been interested in music, especially rap music. He began rapping when he was 12 years old. Although he soon became good enough to make a recording, Will hesitated to do so. At the time, rap music featured a lot of violence. Will was opposed to violence in songs. He could see that violent lyrics had a negative effect on many young listeners.

As he grew older, Will's charm and sense of humor impressed many people. He was offered acting jobs and soon became well-known on his television sitcom, *The Fresh Prince of Bel Air.* Producers of the TV show felt that the part of "the Fresh Prince" fit Will exactly. The show was very successful, and Will lived up to his teacher's nickname.

Will's acting career led to starring roles in major motion pictures. *Independence Day,* which starred Will Smith, earned more money than any movie in 1996. The following year, *Men in Black* earned the most money in 1997. The soundtrack from *Men in Black* gave Will fame as a recording artist. He began mixing both of his interests, music and acting. His new *Men in Black* rock video won the MTV Music Award, while his next film, *Enemy of the State,* thrilled adventure seekers at the movie theaters.

Although Will has enjoyed a tremendous amount of success in his acting career, music is still his first love. He finds singing and writing lyrics much more challenging than acting. Much older now than in his earlier rapping days, Will is not afraid to express what he likes. Will admires intellect in song writing and is confident enough to turn away from lyrics that might have a negative effect on others. Although Will's sense of humor is evident in his music, he often writes songs with meaning and purpose. "Just the Two of Us" is a song he wrote for his young son, Jaden Christopher. Will wants his son to know something about him when he is older. Family and friends are very important to Will. They are what encourage him to continue in his career.

Main Idea

1. Will Smith's talents involve
   a. mathematical abilities.
   b. the art of entertainment.
   c. a combination of sports and humor.

Significant Details

2. Will got his nickname from
   a. his childhood.
   b. his television show.
   c. his rapping career.
3. The film *Independence Day*
   a. showed Will's sense of humor.
   b. earned the most money at the box office.
   c. was a TV comedy.

Drawing Conclusions

4. Will Smith will make a good father for his son because
   a. he knows how to set a good example.
   b. he is very wealthy and can provide his son with whatever he wants.
   c. he will probably let his son star in a music video.

6

MP3391

The Bohemians
(Adapted from a tragic-comic opera *La Boheme* by G. Puccini)

Four struggling young men, the Bohemians, live in an attic studio, or garret, near the Paris Latin Quarter. All are serious about their work, but also know how to enjoy a simple pleasure when they have the chance. One Christmas Eve in 1833, Rudolpho, the writer, looks out the window at the snow-covered roofs while Marcello, the painter, works in a corner. Suddenly, the door bursts open and Colline, the philosopher, with Schaunard, the musician, tramp in with food and drink. The four young men have a merry meal. Then Rudolpho decides he must remain behind to write his newspaper article as the rest of them leave to celebrate the season.

Soon after, Mimi, a beautiful young seamstress living in a nearby attic, knocks at the door. Rudolpho answers and Mimi asks for a light for her candle. The two spend the evening talking and soon realize that they have fallen in love. The next day Rudolpho introduces Mimi to his friends and they all go on a happy shopping trip. Rudolpho buys Mimi a bonnet. They watch a parade. They stop for food and drink. It is a fun afternoon.

Then Mimi and Rudolpho quarrel over a silly incident and decide to part. But Mimi is fatally ill. As the illness gets worse, she wishes to spend her last days near Rudolpho. Rudolpho rushes to her side and sits by her bedside until the end. While the Bohemians dance near the market, Rudolpho mourns his Mimi's sad death.

Main Idea
1. Who were the main characters in the opera?
   a. Rudolpho and Marcello
   b. Rudolpho and Mimi
   c. The Bohemians

Significant Details
2. Since Rudolpho was serious about his work, he was able to meet Mimi. How was this so?
   a. Mimi was a serious writer.
   b. Rudolpho was able to sell his writings to Mimi.
   c. Rudolpho remained home to work when Mimi appeared.

Context Clues
3. Mimi is *fatally ill.*
   a. not seriously ill
   b. illness causing death
   c. ill with influenza

Inference
4. What are two emotions that evolve in a pattern throughout the opera?
   a. seriousness and joy
   b. hatred and pleasure
   c. silliness and fear

Drawing Conclusions
5. How is an opera like a play or movie?

   _____
   _____
   _____
   _____

Following Through
6. Look up opera in the encyclopedia. Find out from which country opera originated. Who were the Camerata and what did they do? What is the difference between an opera and an operetta?

Golda Meir

When Golda and Morris Meyerson arrived in Palestine in 1921, they hoped to find a beautiful and safe retreat. At that time, Jewish people were being treated unfairly in many parts of the world. Golda, and many people like her, wanted a place where Jewish people could live freely. Palestine was to be that Jewish homeland.

But what the Meyersons found was disappointing. The land in Palestine was sandy and desolate. Only a few shacks stood as houses. Worst of all, their Arab neighbors despised the Jews.

Golda didn't despair. Instead, she plunged right into work. The Jews in Palestine soon recognized the talents of hard-working Golda. They persuaded her to work for the government.

For many years, Golda struggled tirelessly for her dream. She helped build hospitals, businesses, highways, farms, and schools in Palestine. She traveled to other countries and spoke to their leaders. Golda tried to make them understand how much the Jewish people wanted their own homeland.

At last the world leaders listened to Golda. On May 14, 1948, the Jews were finally granted independence. The new Jewish state was named Israel. Golda was proud of the work they had done to build this prosperous nation. But their work was not over yet.

Their Arab neighbors immediately declared war on Israel. Golda went into action. For years, she worked without rest towards peace agreements with the Arab nations.

In 1969, Golda Meir (Hebrew for Meyerson) was sworn in as the Premier of Israel. This meant that Golda would now lead the nation that she had struggled all her life to build. Until her death, Golda continued to protect and provide for the Jewish people in their new nation of Israel.

Main Idea
1. What was Golda Meir's dream?
   a. a beautiful new house
   b. a place where her people could live freely
   c. to be ruler of a new nation

Significant Details
2. Who are the Israeli's neighbors?
   a. Arabs
   b. Jews
   c. French

Context Clues
3. The *Premier* of Israel is like the American
   a. Secretary of State.
   b. Bishop.
   c. President.

Inference
4. Golda learned a lot about irrigation and fertilization of soil. Why was this important to Israel? _____
   _____

Drawing Conclusions
5. Why was Golda Meir sometimes referred to as a pioneer?
   _____
   _____

Following Through
6. Look in newspapers or recent magazines. Try to find articles on the Arab-Israeli positions. What is the present relationship between Arabs and Israelis?

The Kibbutz

In Israel, there are several self-sufficient community centers known as *kibbutzim*. They are basically meant to be farming communities. Everyone who lives there, from a young child to an old man, shares in the work. The farming, cooking, repairs, childcare, and decision-making are carried out in common.

Meals, for example, are planned and cooked by both men and women, who take turns in the kitchen. They choose fruits and vegetables from their own fields to prepare. All members of a *kibbutz* eat in the same dining room.

Baby-sitting and teaching may be done by those men and women who are thought to be best at it. A child may stay with an aunt while the mother plows in the field.

The first *kibbutz* was started in 1910 as an experiment by seven farmers. Many people around the world were interested to see if such a plan would work. Today, about five percent of the people in Israel live in *kibbutzim*. They do all repairs, weeding, cleaning, and planting themselves. Sometimes cows or goats are raised, but they are generally sold to buy the necessary products from outside the community.

As *kibbutzim* became more numerous, the communities lost some of the close feeling among the people. More and more *kibbutzim* own factories and plants instead of a more humble shoe repair shop. But the basic idea remains. People work together and try to emphasize equality and the dignity of working with one's hands.

Main Idea
1. A kibbutz is
   a. a school in Israel.
   b. a shoe repair shop.
   c. a community where people work together.

Significant Details
2. Originally, a kibbutz was designed for
   a. farming.
   b. teaching.
   c. raising children.

Context Clues
3. The community is *self-sufficient*.
   a. brings help from the outside
   b. relies on itself
   c. grows vegetables

Inference
4. If new crops were going to be raised on a kibbutz, who would decide which crops to plant?
   a. everyone in the community
   b. the leader of the kibbutz
   c. the women in charge of farming

Drawing Conclusions
5. The main purpose of a kibbutz is to
   a. learn new farming techniques.
   b. give people a sense of equality.
   c. live in Israel.

Following Through
6. Write a report comparing your family to people in a kibbutz. Include chores and decisions which are shared in your family. What might be a disadvantage to living on a kibbutz?

Julie on the Run

Julie's breath came in gasps. She had been running steadily for over twenty minutes. She had to stop and rest. Julie sat down on a small log next to the stream. She tried to think. What would those two men have wanted from the safe?

Julie's father was a NASA engineer, preparing the launch of the next space shuttle. After dinner that evening, he had gone back to work. When he left, Julie wandered into the den to watch TV. Two men were trying to open her father's safe! Before she could stop herself, Julie cried out and the men turned. As they started toward her, she ran out the door, around the house, and darted into the nearby woods. Had they been able to follow her through the thick growth?

Suddenly leaves rustled and a branch cracked. A bird screeched and flew away.

Finish the story. If necessary, continue on another paper.

_____
_____
_____
_____
_____
_____
_____
_____
_____
_____
_____
_____

Ice Golfing

Warm, sunny breezes and clear skies are conditions that bring many golfers out to the golf course. But imagine having your game cancelled because it was too warm! That cancellation happened a few years ago. A golf championship was called off because the April morning was too warm. It was too warm, that is, for ice golfing.

Ice golfing is a fast version of the typical country club golf game. Although the sport is gaining in popularity, there are still not too many places that offer ice golfing. Iceland, Scandinavia, and Greenland offer the best conditions for this sport.

Because of Iceland's proximity to the Northern Lights, Iceland's Arctic Open was played in 24 hours of sunlight. This offers quite an advantage for the golfer. Courses are always open for practice.

Ilulissat, a town 250 miles north of the Arctic Circle, also offers near-perfect conditions for ice golfing. The land is covered with ice and snow and has very few trees or shrubs to interfere with a golf shot.

Uummannaq, another town in northern Greenland, is surrounded by sea ice. This frozen sea makes a fast course for ice golfing.

Because of the sub-zero temperatures, golf shots usually go only short distances. But distance is sometimes made up with a slick skid across the ice. Instead of the usual golf-course hazards like sand traps and water, ice-golf courses offer other challenges. Ice golfers often find themselves doglegging around icebergs rising almost 100 feet in the air.

The putting greens are called "whites" and are areas of smooth, polished ice. Playing on this slick surface takes extra practice. The balls, usually painted in very bright colors, are harder to control on smooth ice. But the course designers anticipated this and made the holes twice as big as regular golf course holes.

Many golfers have played around the world on the lushest, grass courses or the driest, sand courses. But ice golfing offers a new challenge to their skill. Some are anxious to try it. A World Ice Golf Championship has been established in Greenland and the number of competitors is increasing.

continued . . .

11

MP3391

There are still a few problems to be worked out if the regular grass-course golfers are to be persuaded. First, practice time is certainly limited for people who live in the more central part of the world. They do not, after all, have access to ice-golf courses year-round. Secondly, Greenland's traditional counting system only goes to "arqaneq marluk," which means 12. Any numbers over 12 are called "passuit," which means many. Score keeping may be a little difficult if everyone turns in a perfect score of "passuit." Of course different counting systems may be substituted, but it might be tempting to try Greenland's way. Golfers could really keep their scores down!

As different as ice golfing sounds, it still requires skill, determination, and practice. And for many, ice golfing provides a new challenge to an old game.

Main Idea

1. Ice golfing is
   a. a new sport.
   b. played in a rink like ice hockey.
   c. a different version of a familiar sport.

Significant Details

2. You are not likely to find ___ on an ice course.
   a. icebergs
   b. sand traps
   c. frozen snow

Inference

3. The Northern Lights are
   a. near the North Pole.
   b. near the South Pole.
   c. not real.

4. You must be a "good sport" to try ice golfing because
   a. you don't want to lose.
   b. you are likely to make many mistakes.
   c. only the best can play.

Drawing Conclusions

5. What other sport may an ice golfer be willing to try?
   a. broom hockey
   b. track
   c. softball

Edgar Rice Burroughs

Sometimes important people have a town named for them. But not many towns are named for characters out of books. Tarzana, California is headquarters for Tarzan of the Apes, the hero of many books, cartoons, and movies. Tarzan was the son of an English lord. He was abandoned at birth in the jungle and raised by apes. Tarzan's adventures are still popular, even though they were written in 1914. A recent remake of his story, the movie *Greystoke*, was an immediate Hollywood hit.

Edgar Rice Burroughs, the author of the Tarzan books, led an adventurous life himself. At different times, he was a soldier, gold miner, businessman, cowboy, storekeeper, and policeman. Then he wrote the story of Tarzan and became such a success that he spent the rest of his life writing. He published over seventy adventure novels. In addition to crime and western stories, Burroughs gave his readers more and more science fiction tales about lost cities and distant civilizations. In the 1960s, the Tarzan books were reprinted, and captured the imagination of a new generation of readers.

Burroughs' last writing assignment was much different from his futuristic tales. He wrote about an exotic place where he lived for four years during World War II. Burroughs was the oldest of the war correspondents who sent us news from the South Pacific.

Main Idea
1. What made Edgar Rice Burroughs successful?
   a. Burroughs was the son of an English lord.
   b. He made a fortune at gold mining.
   c. He wrote tales of adventure and science fiction.

Significant Details
2. Tarzan's life was spent in
   a. the jungle.
   b. Tarzana, California.
   c. England.

Context Clues
3. Burroughs wrote *futuristic* tales.
   a. western stories
   b. tales of the future
   c. tales of the past
4. An *exotic* place is
   a. strange.
   b. familiar.
   c. boring.

Inference
5. Would people today be interested in stories written over seventy years ago?
   a. No. People like different things today.
   b. Yes. People like to read the same things over again.
   c. Yes. The original Tarzan stories were reprinted in 1960, and rewritten into a popular movie.

Drawing Conclusions
6. What probably made Edgar Rice Burroughs an interesting writer?
   a. He was a soldier, gold miner, and businessman.
   b. He wrote from personal experiences of adventure and exotic places.
   c. He received excellent training in journalism.

Following Through
7. Read *Tarzan of the Apes* by Edgar Rice Burroughs. Compare it with the popular movie *Greystoke*.

Silver and Gold

In 1622, eight Spanish treasure ships were sailing near the Marquesas Islands just west of Key West, Florida. Caught by a sudden hurricane, the ships smashed into the reefs and sank. For over 360 years the ships lay on the bottom of the ocean. Recently, professional treasure hunters discovered one of the eight ships, the "Nuestra Señora de Atocha." They also discovered one of the richest collections of treasure ever uncovered.

Mel Fisher of Treasure A. Salvors, Inc. has spent the last fifteen years searching for sunken ships. Using a combination of computer technology and a homemade "sand scooper," Mel's company led the way to the spectacular find. There is so much treasure that it may take a year to dig it all out and bring it to the surface.

To begin with, there are more than 1,000 bars of silver. Because they are marked with the Spanish King Philip V's tax stamp, they are worth more as bits of history than as money. The Atocha has nearly $400 million in silver, gold, and other treasures stored in the wreckage. The silver bars were the first things to be recovered. People stood around and gasped as the priceless bars were loaded into the backs of worn pickup trucks and old vans.

The treasure was transported to the company office. Fisher has won the right from the government to keep the entire treasure. Once the backers have received their share, crew members will get their portion. It reminds one of the pirate captain splitting the loot with his crew. But this is a legitimate business in which businessmen can earn up to one million dollars in a very interesting way.

Main Idea
1. What successful event has Treasure A. Salvors, Inc. experienced?
   a. It discovered the Spanish King Philip V's tax stamp.
   b. It has earned 1,000 bars of silver.
   c. It discovered a sunken Spanish treasure ship.

Significant Details
2. Who runs Treasure A. Salvors, Inc.?
   a. Mel Fisher.
   b. King Philip.
   c. Señora de Atocha.

Context Clues
3. The silver bars were the first to be *recovered*.
   a. covered again
   b. healthy
   c. retrieved

Inference
4. Could a scuba diver keep treasure he found on the floor of the sea?
   a. Yes, if he were the only person to find it.
   b. Yes, if he has a registered business for the purpose of salvage.
   c. No. All found treasure goes to the local art museum.

Drawing Conclusions
5. Mel Fisher's company will probably continue to be prosperous because
   a. he uses computer technology.
   b. the Atocha has nearly $400 million in treasure.
   c. the company owns eight ships.

Following Through
6. Read about Jean Lafitte, a pirate in the early 1800s. Tell how he might have threatened Mel Fisher's operation if he were alive today.

Thunder on the Mountain
(Adapted from Norse Mythology)

Thor was the Norse god of thunder and lightning. His main goal in life was to defeat the evil giants of the earth who threatened the peaceful lives of gods and men. So Thor spent a great deal of time fighting battles. He was well-equipped for it.

According to Norse legend, Thor rode around in a large chariot. The rumbling of its huge wheels caused the sound of thunder. Lightning was the flash of his magic hammer, which glistened when he threw it at the giants. This hammer, which always went exactly where Thor aimed it, would hit the target and return immediately to his hand. Thor also had iron gloves to catch this red-hot hammer and a wonderful belt that doubled his strength. The hammer, gloves, and belt were all made for him by the friendly dwarfs who lived in the Norse underworld.

Although Thor was willing to fight the enemy, he was friendly and popular in his own home. He lived in a hall, Bilskirnir, that had 540 rooms. He had a beautiful wife, Sif, and two children, Modi, a boy, and Thrud, a girl. Thor was easily aroused from his fireside, however, if anyone reported a giant on the loose. The sudden appearance of a large man with a red beard, great strength, and a desire to protect the little people meant that Thor was in a rage again. Thunder would soon be rumbling from the mountain.

Main Idea
1. Thor devoted his life to
   a. defeating the dwarfs of the underworld.
   b. making thunder and lightning.
   c. protecting his people from evil giants.

Significant Details
2. Thor was known as the god of thunder because of
   a. the noise of his chariot wheels.
   b. his strength.
   c. the thunderstorms he caused.

Context Clues
3. The evil giants *threatened* Thor's people.
   a. teased them
   b. promised them harm
   c. protected them

Inference
4. Is this story fiction or non-fiction? _____
   Explain. _____
   _____
   _____
   _____

Drawing Conclusions
5. How was Thor well-equipped for battle?
   a. He was friendly and popular.
   b. He had a magical hammer, gloves, and a belt.
   c. He lived on top of the mountain, which gave him a clear view of the enemy.

Following Through
6. Get a book on mythology. Find out how other gods and goddesses used their powers.

Julia Morgan

Although she was small and thin as a child, Julia Morgan had very strong ideas on what she wanted to do with her life. Julia grew up in California at the turn of the century. She chose an unusual life for a girl of her times. Julia decided to become an architect, but had to fight all the way to get the training she wanted. With some difficulty, she was admitted to the University of California at Berkeley. It had only a handful of women students at that time. They had no courses in architecture, so she took the closest subject, civil engineering.

Her next step was even more difficult. Encouraged by one of her California professors, Julia traveled to Paris where she tried to enter a famous school of architecture. The professor had not told her that the school rarely allowed women students and certainly not foreign women. Julia kept at the school until she was at last admitted. Male schoolmates made life somewhat uncomfortable for her by pouring water on her, pushing her off benches, and pulling other pranks. Julia, of course, had the last laugh. She was the first woman architect to graduate from Ecole des Beaux-Arts.

Julia did some designing while still in France and then returned home, ready to begin. A movement around the country to help young women was also beginning. Julia, much in tune with this, began designing buildings for the YWCA and other places where women would spend time. Up and down the coast she traveled. Soon Julia became famous for her pure lines, her good use of material, and her ability to make a building blend into the surrounding landscape. She was also very good at balancing two kinds of clients. One might ask for a simple, inexpensive home, while a wealthy client might ask for an elaborate, costly home. She was able to satisfy both types and give them the kind of home they wanted. Her one departure from simple, uncluttered design was the Hearst Castle at San Simeon, California built at the request of William Randolph Hearst.

continued . . .

MP3391

Julia spent nearly all her time working and did not miss social life at all. She met with clients, went to construction sites, and constantly checked the progress of her jobs. It was not unusual for her to lift her long skirts and climb to the top floor to inspect partial construction. If she did not like what she saw, she tore it out with her bare hands.

When Julia retired in 1949, she destroyed all her papers. At her death, she had little in the way of worldly goods. But her legacy to the world was quite generous — nearly 800 buildings — more than any other woman architect in the world had built.

Main Idea
1. Julia Morgan was
   a. a young girl from France.
   b. a civil engineer.
   c. an architect.

Significant Details
2. Julia used simple, clean lines in her designs except for
   a. the YWCA buildings.
   b. the Hearst Castle.
   c. her buildings in Paris.

Context Clues
3. Julia wanted to learn *architecture*.
   a. the study of designing buildings
   b. the study of the French language
   c. selling land and real estate
4. The word *legacy* means about the same as
   a. legal.
   b. prophecy.
   c. gift.

Inference
5. Julia must have been an excellent student because
   a. she took difficult civil engineering classes.
   b. she was the first woman architect to graduate from Ecole des Beaux-Arts.
   c. she traveled up and down the coast.

Drawing Conclusions
6. In addition to her designs of beautiful buildings, Julia's clients admired her because
   a. she used pure lines and natural materials.
   b. she became personally involved in clients' decisions.
   c. she had experience designing in Paris.

Following Through
7. Get a book on becoming an architect. What are the qualifications needed? Make an outline of the steps involved in becoming an **architect**.

MP3391

Hearst Castle

William Randolph Hearst was a wealthy American publisher and politician. His parents had left him 250,000 acres of land in San Simeon, California. This land afforded a view of the Pacific Ocean to the west, and majestic mountains to the east. William and his family often went there to camp. But in 1919, William became tired of camping out in the open. He met with an architect, Julia Morgan, and told her he would like to build a little something.

The "little something" Hearst and Morgan eventually built was one of the most lavish and spectacular estates in the country. He called the estate La Cuesta Encantada, which means The Enchanted Hill. The place is also known as Hearst Castle.

William had been collecting art treasures and ideas since his first visit to Europe. La Casa Grande, the main house on the estate, is the perfect setting for his vast collection of art work. In fact, most of this house was designed specifically to accommodate the art. With its rising twin towers and intricate carvings, La Casa Grande does indeed look like a castle. There are over one hundred rooms in the house, including a movie theater. Every room is adorned with Hearst's art objects, paintings, and fine furniture.

The three guest houses on the hill look like miniature castles. Each has its own terraces and gardens.

Behind the main house is the immense indoor swimming pool known as the Roman pool. The walls of this huge building are set with rich blue mosaic tiles and are trimmed in gold. Two narrow staircases lead to the second floor where an arched diving platform overlooks the pool. On the roof of the building are tennis courts.

continued . . .

MP3391

One of the most breathtaking sights on the estate is the outdoor pool, known as Neptune's pool. With white marble columns surrounding it, the pool lends itself to Hearst's collection of marble statues. One group of French statues is set right in the shallow end of the water.

Along the main road is Hearst's private zoo. Among his exotic animals are water buffalo, chimpanzees, yak, elephants, tigers, zebra, and ostriches. Hearst also had stables where he raised Arabian horses. The kennels behind the house had about eighty well-cared for dachshunds and terriers.

When William Hearst died, Mrs. Hearst donated the estate to the California park system. Since 1958, nearly one million visitors drive up California's coastal highway to tour La Cuesta Encantada each year.

Main Idea
1. What is La Cuesta Encantada?
   a. a Spanish mission
   b. a luxurious residence
   c. an art gallery

Significant Details
2. The house was designed specifically to accommodate
   a. many people.
   b. lost treasure.
   c. art work.

Context Clues
3. The estate is one of the most *lavish* in the country.
   a. fancy
   b. large
   c. practical

Inference
4. Why didn't Hearst open an art museum and display his treasures there?

   _____

   _____

Drawing Conclusions
5. Some people have called the Hearst Castle "a rich man's plaything." Why?

   _____

   _____

Following Through
6. Imagine you owned several acres of land. Design a home you would build for yourself. What would you include? Draw plans for your home. Try to estimate the cost of building your home.

Ghost of Blanton Hall

In New Jersey in the late 1800s, there was a boys' school, Blanton Hall, that stood at the top of a tall hill. Nearby was a river with strong currents. Although parents admired the school for its teaching, the boys liked the sports as well. Each year, the big sport event was the rowing race with several schools. Their biggest rival was Gainsville, a similar school in New York.

About a week before the 1873 contest with Gainsville, a strange thing happened. After dinner one night, most of the boys were relaxing or reading in the main hall. Suddenly, Will jumped up and shouted, "Look! At the window!"

All the boys turned to the large window. Outside stood the ghostly figure of a young boy. His long hair was wet, his fine clothes were smeared with mud, and his face looked very sad. By the time the boys had rushed to the window, the figure had vanished. Many times during that week, the sad little figure appeared at a window. Once, a younger boy met it on the stairs. He was so frightened that he ran to his room and would not get out of bed for two days.

continued . . .

The school professors and other town scholars began to check into old records. They found that there had been a young boy of that same description at the school many years before. He had been a champion rower, but one year during the race against Gainsville, he fell overboard. His body was never found. The rowing coach realized that Blanton Hall had never beaten Gainsville since that time.

The night before the 1873 contest, the dripping boy was seen in three different places around the school. The students were definitely getting nervous, but went on with their plans for the race. The day of the contest was bright and clear. At 8:00 a.m., the race began. Possibly the sad little ghost was helping them, because that year, Blanton Hall rowers won the race. The boy with the dripping hair was never seen again.

Main Idea
1. Who was the ghost of Blanton Hall?
   a. a young student from Gainsville
   b. a champion rower from Blanton Hall
   c. an old man who used to own Blanton Hall

Significant Details
2. What happened at the race in 1873?
   a. Blanton Hall rowers won the race.
   b. A young rower fell overboard.
   c. The ghost appeared.

Context Clues
3. Gainsville's team was their biggest *rival*.
   a. a team that has never been beaten
   b. a team of champion rowers
   c. a team you would most like to beat

Inference
4. Do you think the ghost of Blanton Hall will be seen again? Why or why not?

_____

Drawing Conclusions
5. Some people don't believe ghost stories. Were the boys at Blanton Hall able to convince others of their stories?
   a. Yes. School professors checked old records.
   b. No. The other teammates would not row with them.
   c. Yes. The town scholars saw the ghost, too.

Following Through
6. Get a book on ghosts or poltergeists. Find out what is used as evidence to support ghost sightings.

MP3391

White Water Rafting

Jason grabbed the side of the rubber raft as a huge wave of churning white water crashed towards him! "Pull, one-two," shouted the raft guide. Jason jammed his oar into the water and paddled as the guide commanded. Another wave, this one bigger and faster, pounded against the raft and lifted it out of the water. Again the raft guide shouted commands. Jason paddled furiously until the raft was through the wave and into calm water. Jason put down his oar and smiled to himself. He was finally doing what he had always wanted to do — ride the rapids of the Colorado River.

Although the river ride was a scary one, Jason knew they were safe. The large, inflatable raft was strong. Jason and the nine other passengers in the raft wore sturdy life jackets. Most important, Charlie, their raft guide, was an experienced river runner.

Snow-capped mountains rose from the river banks. As the raft floated along with the strong current, Jason looked up at the mountains and thought about early explorers.

"Imagine what it must have been like to discover this river," he thought to himself. "In those days, the explorers had to be their own guides. . . ."

continued . . .

MP3391

Jason's thoughts were interrupted by a low, steady roar. The river turned around a bend and, up ahead, the rapids beat furiously over huge rocks in the river. "Okay, everybody," shouted the guide. "Get ready!"

Jason tightened his muscles and listened for Charlie's commands. "Pull, one-two. Pull left, harder!" The foaming water did indeed look white. Swirling waves hurled the raft closer to the rapids. The roar was so loud Jason could barely hear Charlie. "Stay left," the guide called. "Watch out for the rocks! Pull, one-two."

Suddenly they were in the rapids, bouncing up and down off the waves and rocks. Jason felt like he was riding a wet roller coaster. "Hang on!" yelled Charlie. A huge wave poured over the side, almost sweeping Jason into the rapids. And then the river widened and the rapids dropped. They had made it through!

Jason looked at the other drenched passengers and grinned. "We did it!" they shouted together. "We tamed the wild Colorado River!"

Main Idea
1. On what kind of trip was Jason?

_____

Significant Details
2. The raft was made of
   a. water.
   b. rubber.
   c. strong cloth.

Context Clues
3. The raft was *inflatable*.
   a. rubber
   b. made out of water
   c. able to be blown up with air

Inference
4. Where would rapids in the river occur?
   a. where the river widens
   b. where the river narrows
   c. where the river flows into the ocean

Drawing Conclusions
5. Why was the trip a scary one? _____

_____

_____

_____

Following Through
6. Get a book about rivers in America. Find out which rivers are good for river rafting and which are good for canoeing.

23 MP3391

Ansel Adams

Ansel Easton Adams is considered one of the best photographers of the American West. Ansel didn't just take photographs, he "made" them. That was the key to Ansel's success. To him, a photograph was not just a snapshot; it was a true expression of something.

When Ansel was a young boy in San Francisco, his father bought him a pass to the Panama-Pacific World's Fair. Ansel went to the fair every day. He was fascinated by the exhibits of modern art. But it wasn't until a year later that Ansel's own art career was launched. Ansel's family went on a vacation to Yosemite National Park. The beauty of the mountain landscape made a strong impression on Ansel. It was there that he took his first photograph.

After that trip, Ansel returned to Yosemite Valley every year. He wanted to make a "visual diary" that would show nature's beauty unspoiled by man.

From the start, Ansel's black and white photographs were very good. It wasn't long before his pictures were recognized by other artists and photographers. With the help of these artists, Ansel's photographs were published in books and displayed in art galleries.

continued . . .

MP3391

Ansel became known for his "straight photography" approach. He didn't like other photographers who used trick lighting, fancy props, and retouching in their pictures. He liked to make pictures of things exactly as they were. Ansel used the natural lighting of the sun to help him get interesting effects in his photos. Sometimes Ansel would get up at sunrise to make a picture of a mountain or waterfall. Then he would wait all day until the sun was almost about to set, and make the same picture again. The difference in the sun's angle would make the same scene look completely different.

It was this use of light in photography that made Ansel famous. Many art students tried to copy his techniques. Ansel helped these students by writing books and teaching classes on lighting in photography. He started the first department of photography at the Museum of Modern Art in New York. Later, he did the same at the California School of Fine Arts in San Francisco.

Ansel felt that his pictures helped people to understand and appreciate nature and their environment. Making these sharp, detailed, and dramatic photographs was Ansel's way of preserving America's wilderness.

Main Idea
1. Ansel Adams was a
    a. photographer.
    b. young boy.
    c. film maker.

Significant Details
2. What made Ansel's work famous?
    a. retouching techniques
    b. pictures of beautiful mountains
    c. use of natural light in photography

Context Clues
3. Ansel Adam's *visual diary* was
    a. a diary he wrote in every day.
    b. pictures he took of his surroundings.
    c. a record of how many mountains he climbed.

Inference
4. Would Ansel prefer to take pictures indoors or outdoors? Explain.

    _____

    _____

_____

_____

_____

_____

_____

Drawing Conclusions
5. Ansel was different from other photographers because
    a. of his straight photography approach.
    b. of his trick photography.
    c. his pictures were displayed in art galleries.

Following Through
6. Get some photography books by Ansel Adams. Try to see what made his pictures unique. Some of his books are *Born Free and Equal, The Islands of Hawaii, Ansel Adams, Images 1923-1974,* and *The Portfolios of Ansel Adams.*

MP3391

What's a Chunnel?

The English Channel is an arm of the Atlantic Ocean that lies south of England. Large waves from the main body of water are squeezed into this small area, causing choppy waters and difficult sailing. The English Channel separates England and France. Although the distance between the two countries is not far, the Channel is often hard to cross because of dense fog and high seas. For many years, people had been talking about a tunnel under the Channel.

Several attempts were made to build such a tunnel. Although walls were shored up for the tunnel, political disputes caused the projects to be abandoned. Finally, government leaders from France and Britain agreed to let the tunnel construction proceed without interference from either country.

But decisions still had to be made. Tunnels as long as 30 miles had been built on land, but underwater tunnels were usually just a few miles long. This tunnel would have to be extra wide because train tracks were to be incorporated in the design. Some began to wonder if the project could be done. Who would work on the project? The tunnel would connect both England and France, and workers from each country would speak different languages. Who would interpret? Who would be in charge? On which side would the project start?

Finally, the decisions were made, billions of dollars were spent, and the "Chunnel," as it was called, became a reality. Now, millions of commuters use the Chunnel each year. Shuttle trains, about half a mile long, carry vehicles on rail tracks through the underwater tunnel.

Passenger trains, tourists' vehicles, and freight vehicles travel through the Chunnel without interference from weather, foggy conditions, or dangerous waters.

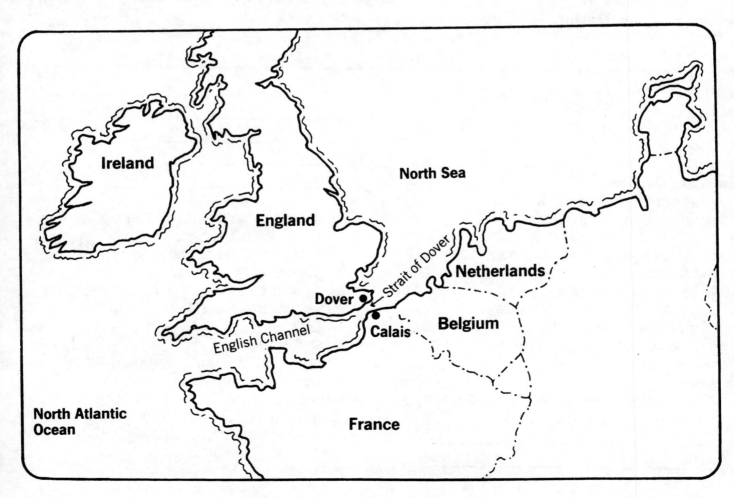

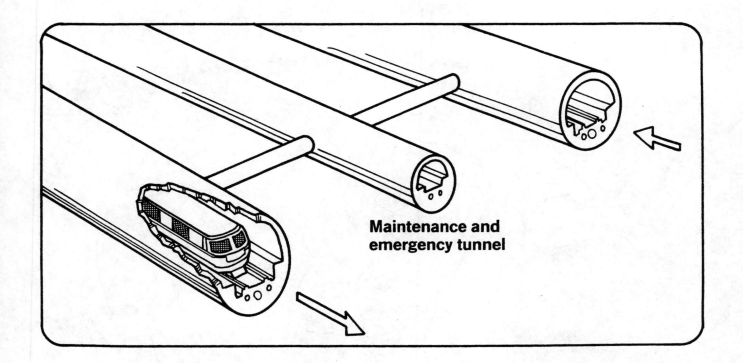

Maintenance and emergency tunnel

Main Idea

1. What is the Chunnel?
   a. a bridge across the English Channel
   b. a tunnel under the English Channel
   c. an artificial island

Significant Details

2. The English Channel is between
   a. France and England.
   b. England and Ireland.
   c. Germany and England.

Context Clues

3. The project was abandoned for *political* reasons.
   a. reasons determined by the government
   b. reasons determined by bridge builders
   c. reasons determined by England

Inference

4. What problem may have arisen when building the Chunnel?
   a. Trains might not be able to fit through it.
   b. Only people from England would be allowed to use the tunnel.
   c. A decision would have to be made as to which country would pay for the tunnel.

Drawing Conclusions

5. The Chunnel would be helpful because it would
   a. be the only way to get from England to France.
   b. offer another traveling method.
   c. help drain the Strait of Dover.

Following Through

6. Get a book on swimming records. Find out how many people have been successful in swimming across the English Channel.

Aladdin's Lamp
(From *The Arabian Nights*)

Aladdin, the son of a poor widow, lived in one of China's wealthy cities. A magician from Africa arrived in that city one day. He had a new plan and needed a young man's help. The magician saw Aladdin on the street and decided he was just the right person to help. He pretended to be Aladdin's long lost uncle. Aladdin's mother was surprised when her son brought home this unknown "uncle," but was happy to receive the gold pieces he gave her for food.

The magician then dressed Aladdin in fine clothes and promised to set him up in business. First, however, he wished to show Aladdin something. Aladdin accompanied the magician out of the city and into a lonely spot. The magician lit a fire, spoke some magic words and behold! — a hidden door appeared in the ground. Following the magician's instructions, Aladdin pulled the heavy door open and found steps leading to a cave below. The magician told him to enter the cave.

First he gave Aladdin a magic ring, which would keep harm away. Then he told him to walk carefully, without touching any walls, through three underground rooms until he reached the one with a lamp. Aladdin was to take the lamp, empty its oil, and return to his "uncle." All went well until Aladdin returned to the foot of the steps with the lamp. The magician told Aladdin to hand him the lamp. Aladdin would not give the magician the dusty old lamp until he first held out a hand to help Aladdin up the steps. The magician, who cared only about the lamp, grew angry, slammed the door, and locked Aladdin in the dark cave.

Aladdin stayed in the cave for two days without food or water. Then by accident, he rubbed the magic ring on his finger. Instantly, a large genie stood before him.

continued . . .

MP3391

"What can I do for you, master?" asked the figure. "I am the genie of the ring."

"Oh, take me home," answered Aladdin.

Immediately Aladdin, still clutching the lamp, was at his front door. His mother was very glad to see him, but sorry she had no food for him. Aladdin was very hungry and told her to sell the lamp and buy food. She began to rub the lamp to clean some of the dust away. Pouf! An even larger genie appeared from the lamp.

"I am the genie of the lamp," it said. "What are your wishes?"

Aladdin, much astonished, nevertheless had sense enough to ask for food. A magnificent dinner was soon set before him. As the days went by, the genie provided very well for Aladdin. He soon had new clothes, a fine horse, and even won the hand of a lovely princess in marriage. With the help of the genie, he built a marble palace for his new wife. Because of his kindness to those around him, Aladdin became a happy and loved citizen.

In Africa, the magician heard that Aladdin, instead of being dead in a cave, was happily married. The angry magician set out at once for China. Ah ... but that is another story.

Main Idea
1. Aladdin was
   a. a famous magician.
   b. a Chinese princess.
   c. the son of a poor widow.

Significant Details
2. Aladdin went into the underground cave to get
   a. his uncle.
   b. a lamp.
   c. new clothing.

Context Clues
3. When Aladdin *accompanied* the magician, that meant he
   a. opened the door for the magician.
   b. walked with the magician.
   c. left the magician at the top of the cave steps.

Inference
4. Which do you think is the best answer? The magician was a
   a. dishonest man.
   b. stupid man.
   c. generous man.

Drawing Conclusions
5. The lamp genie appeared when
   a. Aladdin needed him.
   b. the magician was not looking.
   c. Aladdin rubbed the lamp.

Following Through
6. Scheherazade, a character in the *Arabian Nights*, saved her life by telling a story each night to the sultan. She always stopped at the most exciting part and the sultan let her live so he could hear the end. Read the story of Aladdin and find out how it ends. Or write your own ending to this story.

MP3391

Isaac Asimov

Isaac Asimov was a gifted scientist and writer. He wrote over three hundred books and his work appeared in thousands of magazines. His books range from joke books to science textbooks. In fact, he probably wrote more different kinds of books than any other author in America.

Isaac's favorite kind of writing was science fiction. His interest in science fiction began when he was young. Isaac was born in Russia in 1920. His family moved to the United States when he was three years old. His father started his own business in the United States. Mr. Asimov sold candy, newspapers, and magazines. While helping his father in the store, Isaac read all the new science fiction magazines in stock.

Mr. Asimov did not want Isaac to read the magazines. He thought the extra reading would interfere with Isaac's schoolwork. But Mr. Asimov soon changed his mind. Isaac proved to be a brilliant student. He was able to devour the magazines, taking notes and keeping files on the stories, and still keep up with his school work. Isaac learned so well that he was able to enter high school when he was only twelve years old.

While continuing his education, Isaac began writing his own science fiction stories. His story, "Nightfall," was voted one of the best science fiction stories of all times. Isaac earned his doctorate degree in chemistry and began teaching. All the while, he continued to write successfully. His fictional plots based on accurate scientific theories account for much of his success. His stories might really happen. After he published "The Foundation Trilogy," three stories about the Galactic Empire, Isaac decided to make writing a full-time career.

Asimov's writing is for both children and adults. He was known for making scientific and technological material easier to understand for the general reader. He wrote on many other topics, including the Bible and Shakespeare. He even wrote about himself in two autobiographies. But Isaac's true love among all his work was science fiction. Isaac died in 1992, but left many unpublished tales of science fiction. Readers and fans can still look forward to more of Isaac Asimov's exciting stories.

Main Idea

1. Isaac Asimov is best known as a
   a. Russian immigrant.
   b. brilliant science fiction author.
   c. great chemistry teacher.

Significant Details

2. Which Asimov story was voted the best science fiction story?
   a. "Nightfall"
   b. "I, Robot"
   c. "The Foundation Trilogy"

3. Which of his works marked the turning point in Isaac's career?
   a. "Nightfall"
   b. "I, Robot"
   c. "The Foundation Trilogy"

4. Isaac's father
   a. ran a store.
   b. wrote books.
   c. taught school.

Context Clues

5. When Isaac *devoured* the magazines, he
   a. read them completely.
   b. ate them very quickly.
   c. took notes on them.

6. An *autobiography* is
   a. a fictional story written by an author.
   b. a story a person writes about his or her own life.
   c. the story of a famous person's life written by someone else.

Inference

7. Why did Isaac give up his interest in science?
   a. He found he was a better writer than scientist.
   b. He didn't. He was able to combine science and writing.
   c. His father did not want him to be a scientist.

8. Isaac could make scientific material easy to understand. Why do you think this is so?
   a. He could not speak English.
   b. He studied Shakespeare.
   c. He knew a lot about science.

Drawing Conclusions

9. If Isaac Asimov wrote the following books, which do you think would have been his favorite?
   a. *Animal Stories from the Far East*
   b. *High Scorers of Pro Football*
   c. *Life on Planet Krypton*

Following Through

10. Read a short story written by Isaac Asimov. Now read a story written by H.G. Wells, an earlier writer. Write a paragraph comparing the two stories. How are they alike? How are they different? Which do you prefer?

The Water Clock

Long ago people often used a sundial, or shadow clock, to give them some idea of the time of day. They could tell ten o'clock in the morning from three o'clock in the afternoon. At night or on a cloudy day, however, the sun did not cast a shadow. At those times, people could not use a sundial.

Around 1600 B.C., the Egyptians created a water clock, or *clepsydra*. This was a much more exact way of measuring time. The clepsydra was a large bowl that often had carvings or paintings on the outside. There were holes in the bottom of the bowl. Water dripped through them steadily. Inside the bowl, there were markings every inch or so. These marks were spaced to measure a certain length of time. As the water dripped from the bowl, the water level dropped. The amount of water still in the bowl showed the time of day. Many kinds of water clocks were later used by the Greeks, Romans, Arabs, and Chinese.

Recently a number of ancient Egyptian treasures were brought to the United States. They were shown in Memphis, Tennessee, a sister city of Memphis, Egypt. Some of them dated back to the time of an important

Egyptian pharaoh. His name was Ramses the Great. One of the treasures was a wonderful water clock. It was made of alabaster, a smooth, white stone. The ancient markings could still be seen inside the bowl. There were faded paintings on the outside of the bowl. Despite all of our modern clocks, the Egyptian water clock, thousands of years old, dripped on to let visitors know the time of day.

Main Idea
1. The most important thing in this story is
   a. a Chinese exhibition.
   b. an Egyptian invention.
   c. a river in Tennessee.

Significant Details
2. A clepsydra is
   a. a sundial.
   b. a modern watch.
   c. a water clock.
3. The water clock was first used
   a. by Egyptians.
   b. in the United States.
   c. in space.

Context Clues
4. A *pharaoh* is
   a. a large ship.
   b. an alabaster bowl.
   c. the ruler of a country.

Inference
5. Alabaster must be very hard because
   a. it has lasted for thousands of years.
   b. it will not break if dropped.
   c. the pharaohs built ships from it.

Following Through
6. Look up "Egypt" in the encyclopedia. List some of the other materials used by Egyptians to make beautiful art objects.

The Camp-Out

Mike and Larry felt excited as they packed their camping gear. They had finally persuaded their parents to let them camp out alone. They would camp at Uncle Jim's farm as they had in the past. This time, however, *they* would decide where to set up the tent.

After leaving the house, Mike and Larry looked and looked for the perfect spot. They found a cool place under shady trees in the field farthest from the farmhouse. It was next to an old cornfield. By the time the two boys had put up the tent, it was almost dark. They were so tired that they fell asleep almost as soon as they zipped up their sleeping bags.

It was still very dark when Larry woke Mike. "Did you hear that? Someone is calling for help," Larry said.

"I didn't hear anything," said Mike, as he struggled out of his sleeping bag.

"Come on," said Larry. "It sounds like someone is in the cornfield."

Yawning and grumbling, Mike picked up the flashlight and followed Larry out of the tent. They pulled aside bushes and weeds. Then they opened the rusted gate leading into the cornfield. Suddenly, they were in a different world. A spooky light shone all around, making it as bright as daylight. They saw black, bare trees without a single leaf. There were wiggly, gray plants growing from the ground. Dark red water bubbled in a stream lined with big, purple rocks.

"Where are we? What happened to the cornfield?" whispered Mike.

Finish the story. If necessary, continue on another piece of paper.

_____
_____
_____
_____
_____
_____
_____
_____
_____
_____
_____
_____
_____
_____
_____
_____

MP3391

Langston Hughes

Young Langston Hughes loved music. He often made up words in his mind to match blues melodies that he enjoyed. But Langston did not think of these words as poetry. He gave no real thought to poetry until he was in the eighth grade in Lincoln, Illinois. Langston was one of two blacks in the class. He was well liked and was a good student. When class officers were chosen, the students elected Langston to be class poet.

Langston was pleased with the honor, but he did not know that he would really have to write a poem. As graduation came closer, Langston learned that he not only had to write a poem, but he also had to read it at the graduation ceremony.

"My first poem was about the longest I ever wrote—sixteen verses," said Langston later. The first half of the poem praised the teachers. The second half praised his classmates.

That poem was the beginning of a long and remarkable literary career for young Hughes. He was born in Joplin, Missouri, in 1902. His family moved around the country as he grew up. Later, Langston traveled to other countries: Mexico, Spain, and parts of Europe. Sometimes the family had little money. Other times they had plenty.

Langston worked at a variety of jobs in many places, but there was always time for writing. He saw poor people, rich people, happy people, hard times, and wonderful times. Much of his writing told of people or things he had seen as he traveled.

Langston was sometimes called the "poet of his people." His work showed a realistic picture of the lives of black Americans. He also had a wonderful gift of humor. It, too, worked its way into his poetry and plays. He combined fun and sadness in such a moving way that many humorists tried to copy his style. Langston's poems have been translated into six languages, and many have been set to music. In 1960, Langston was awarded the Spingarn Medal. This honor is given to a black person who has reached the highest achievement in his or her field.

Main Idea
1. Langston Hughes was known mainly for his
   a. blues music.
   b. fine poetry.
   c. sense of fun.

Significant Details
2. How long was Langston's first poem?
   a. sixteen lines
   b. sixteen pages
   c. sixteen verses
3. Langston was awarded
   a. a scholarship.
   b. a trip to Spain.
   c. the Spingarn Medal.

Context Clues
4. A *humorist* is someone who
   a. sings and dances.
   b. writes or tells funny stories.
   c. lets others have their own way.
5. His work was *realistic*.
   a. true to life
   b. very pretty
   c. printed many times

Following Through
6. Find a book with poems by Langston Hughes. Read two poems. Decide whether they are happy, sad, or both. Write a paragraph about one poem.

MP3391

A New Home for African Art

Ancient African art objects were made hundreds of years before Europeans came to Africa. Until the turn of this century, very few people who lived outside of Africa knew anything at all about its works of art. But now people from all over the world are admiring and appreciating African art.

Many pieces of African art are masks. There are many kinds of masks and many reasons that the Africans wore them. Most masks are carved from wood or ivory. They are usually painted, and some have shells, beads, and feathers on them.

Some African art was made to be used for a purpose. Hunters' spears were carefully made for killing animals. Sometimes lions or other game animals were carved on the spearheads. The hunters that made the spears believed that this gave them power over the animals they killed.

Early sculpture is usually thought to be Africa's best art. Some statues are very lifelike. Others are just outlines of a person or animal. Each tribe decorated its statues with its own style.

With such variety, it is easy to see how the study of African art can become complicated. Some cities provide special places for exhibits of African art, but usually the art is included with works from other nations. At the Smithsonian Institute's complex in Washington, D.C., there is a beautiful new building, the National Museum of African Art. It is the only place in the country dedicated just to the artistic heritage of black people. Although the museum is partially underground, it is big and bright. Here, at last, is a place where those who wish to study African art can find the proper information. The museum is a place for thinking as well as for looking. And it is a place for some to seek their roots.

Main Idea
1. This story is mainly about
   a. chasing witches.
   b. decorated spears.
   c. African art.

Significant Details
2. African masks are usually
   a. carved from wood or ivory.
   b. used to frighten children.
   c. decorated with lions.
3. The new building in Washington, D.C. is called
   a. the Smithsonian Institute.
   b. the Capitol Building.
   c. the National Museum of African Art.
4. Part of the new building is
   a. gold.
   b. marble.
   c. underground.

Context Clues
5. An *exhibit* is something like a
   a. show.
   b. mask.
   c. statue.
6. In this story, *complex* means
   a. difficult.
   b. a group of buildings.
   c. a collection of art.

Drawing Conclusions
7. Why do you think many people will visit this new building?
   a. Africans like to visit museums.
   b. This is the only museum just for African art.
   c. The building won an architectural prize.

MP3391

About the Invisible Man

The Invisible Man, by H. G. Wells, is a science fiction story written in the late 1800s. The story is about an evil and selfish man named Griffin. After years of study and experiments, he discovered a way to make himself invisible. Griffin was very pleased with this discovery. He could steal without leaving a trace. He could rob people's homes without the fear of being caught. He made many plans as he dreamed of his new life of riches.

But Griffin had not thought about the problems of being invisible. Although his body could not be seen, it still needed to be clothed and fed like any other body. Griffin lived in London, where the weather was often cool and damp. He needed clothes and shoes but soon found that they were hard to steal. People would not notice him, but they would notice clothing flying away. Food was another problem. Griffin had made his stomach invisible, but not the food going into it. He had to hide himself when he ate.

Finally, Griffin disguised himself. He wore a big coat, scarves, bandages, and sunglasses. He was able to pass as a man who had been badly hurt. He rented a room in a boardinghouse and began working on his experiment again. But the townspeople soon discovered his secret. While he was trying to get away, Griffin damaged the house and hurt several people. Soon people all over were searching for him.

As Griffin ran from town to town, he became more ruthless and evil. He killed almost anyone who crossed his path. Finally, his terrible way of life caught up with him. The experiment which he thought would bring him a life of riches and happiness only brought him a cruel and lonely death.

Main Idea
1. The invisible man's life was
   a. happy and rich.
   b. full of funny events.
   c. full of hiding and terror.

Significant Details
2. *The Invisible Man* was written by
   a. H.G. Wells.
   b. Griffin.
   c. a man in London.
3. Griffin hoped his experiment would
   a. make him wealthy.
   b. make him well known.
   c. make him a better scientist.

Context Clues
4. Griffin became more *ruthless.*
   a. invisible
   b. mean
   c. wealthy

Inference
5. Why did the townspeople want to catch Griffin?
   a. They wanted to see an invisible person.
   b. They wanted to punish him.
   c. They wanted to get rich too.

Drawing Conclusions
6. What lesson does this story teach?
   a. Be satisfied with what you have.
   b. Don't count your chickens before they hatch.
   c. Be careful with science experiments.

Sequoya and the Talking Leaves

Sequoya, a Cherokee Indian, became a true hero to his people. Although he was a fine hunter and trader, he is not remembered for these skills. He is known for his skill as a linguist, an expert in languages.

Sequoya was born in Tennessee in 1760. His mother was Cherokee, and his father was white. He grew up among the Cherokees and knew no English. When he was older and began to trade and travel for the tribe, Sequoya learned to speak French, Spanish, and English. He also became very interested in the white man's way of writing. He saw how useful it was to be able to send a written message to someone many miles away. The young man decided to develop a system of writing for the Cherokees. Sequoya worked long and hard. He carved symbols with his knife onto pieces of bark.

It took twelve years, but Sequoya did finish a system of writing for his own people. He used letters from the English alphabet along with other symbols and made each stand for a syllable in the Cherokee language. There were a total of eighty-six symbols. This type of system is called a syllabary. With this new language, or "talking leaves" as the Cherokees called it, they were able to write to other members of the tribe. They read books in their own language and printed a

Cherokee newspaper. Most important of all, they wrote down facts about unique Cherokee customs and lives.

In his later years, Sequoya traveled to Washington, D.C., and to the West to fight for the rights of all Native Americans. After his death in 1843, Sequoya received a well-earned honor. The giant redwood tree, the sequoia, as well as Sequoia National Park in California were named for him. A large statue of him was placed in Statue Hall in Washington, D.C. Sequoya and his "talking leaves" have made permanent marks on history.

Main Idea
1. This story is mainly about
   a. Sequoia National Park.
   b. the invention of a written language.
   c. English alphabet symbols.

Significant Details
2. How many symbols were in Sequoya's syllabary?
   a. hundreds
   b. twelve
   c. eighty-six
3. The sequoia is
   a. a giant redwood tree.
   b. a branch of red leaves.
   c. an alphabet.

Context Clues
4. A *symbol* is something like a
   a. kind of tree.
   b. piece of art.
   c. letter or number.
5. Anything that is *unique* is
   a. old.
   b. one of a kind.
   c. written by hand.
6. A person who is a *linguist* is
   a. a forest worker.
   b. a language expert.
   c. an Indian leader.

Mickey Mouse Gardening

At Disney World, you are likely to see a Minnie Mouse bush or a Pluto tree. Each has been carefully shaped to look like the Disney characters. Animals, dinosaurs, monsters, and other cartoon favorites are formed from plants and trees.

Disney World hires the best horticulturists and landscapers to work in their gardens. Topiary plants are probably the hardest to grow. Topiary gardening is a way of training trees and bushes to grow in certain shapes. It takes a long time for a topiary plant to take shape. It is not unusual for a bush to take three to five years to grow into its planned shape. A tall giraffe tree might take ten years to reach its proper size. While the bush is growing gardeners must carefully cut and trim the branches to fit the shape of a certain character.

An easier way of getting a plant to take shape is by using chicken wire. The wire is bent into a shape and then filled with a plant called moss. Next, vines are planted in the moss. Vines are perfect for this kind of

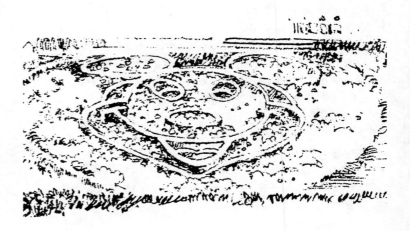

gardening because they grow quickly. They can also be trained to go in any direction. They follow the chicken wire form, and soon a whole plant shape is ready. The wire forms look very much like Mickey and Minnie do in cartoons because they are planned by the same artists who draw the cartoons. The gardens at Disney World are filled with plant-like cartoon characters!

Main Idea
1. Topiary gardening is a
   a. way to grow animals.
   b. way of training plants.
   c. way of growing tall trees.

Significant Details
2. At Disney World, you might see a plant shaped like a
   a. monster.
   b. car.
   c. chicken.
3. A quick-growing plant used in topiary gardening is
   a. moss.
   b. a shrub.
   c. a vine.
4. In topiary gardening, most plants grow into their planned shape in
   a. 3 to 5 weeks.
   b. 3 to 5 months.
   c. 3 to 5 years.

5. The chicken-wire plants really look like Disney characters because
   a. Walt Disney planned them.
   b. the TV characters posed for them.
   c. they were planned by the Disney artists.

Context Clues
6. A *horticulturist* is
   a. someone who draws cartoon characters.
   b. someone who works with plants.
   c. the person who runs Disney World.

Drawing Conclusions
7. Why might Pinnochio be a good choice as a Disney topiary plant?
   a. He is a very small character.
   b. He is a puppet made of wood and would do well outdoors.
   c. His nose could grow quickly or be cut at will.

MP3391

Close Encounter

Can you imagine being stranded on a raft surrounded by sharks in the middle of an ocean? Two sisters, Laurie and Sherie Dobbs, went through this long and frightening experience.

The two girls were on vacation with their family. They were staying in Alabama, on the Gulf of Mexico. They had stayed at their hotel before so they knew the area. One morning, the sisters brought a seven-foot, inflatable raft to the shore. They planned to rest, catch up on each other's news, and work on their tans. They put the raft in the water near the shore, where the water was just up to their knees. Then they lay down on their backs to chat and soak up some sun. A short time later, Sherie turned over and discovered that the raft had traveled an incredible amount. It had floated so far out into the gulf, land was barely visible!

The raft had evidently been caught by an outgoing tide, and within twenty minutes, the girls could no longer see land. They began to paddle with their hands, trying to turn the raft and steer it in the right direction. Working against strong water currents, they did not go far. The sun rose higher in the sky, and the girls began to suffer from the heat. They splashed water on their shoulders to get cooler. That was a big mistake.

Suddenly, sharks appeared around the raft. At first there were just a few sharks, then more and more came near. The water was so clear that the girls could see the sharks from head to tail. The sharks began to bump the raft. Either they were playing or they had far more deadly intentions. The girls were sure the sharks were trying to overturn the raft. They tried their best to be brave. Sherie was very frightened. Laurie was afraid too, but she tried to calm her sister. They hoped that by that time someone had reported them missing.

The hotel reported the missing raft. The nearby Coast Guard station sent up an observation plane and launched a search boat. The girls heard the plane and began flashing a shiny mat they had brought with them. The pilot saw their signal and radioed the Naval Air Station. Within a short time, a Navy helicopter arrived. The air current from the propellers scared the sharks away. A diver jumped into the water to help the girls into the lift.

continued . . .

The helicopter took them to a hospital for a checkup. Except for burned shoulders resulting from six hours in the sun, the girls recovered almost immediately. They were soon resting in their hotel room with their family. The family plans to return again for future vacations. It is almost certain, however, that from now on their sunbathing will be done on the beach.

Main Idea

1. This story is mainly about
   a. an inflatable raft.
   b. a frightening experience.
   c. a Naval Air Force base.

Significant Details

2. Laurie and Sherie were stranded
   a. in a lake.
   b. for twenty minutes.
   c. for six hours.

3. The Coast Guard sent
   a. an observation plane.
   b. a helicopter.
   c. an extra raft.

4. The girls were frightened by
   a. their family.
   b. sharks.
   c. a diver.

Context Clues

5. The Coast Guard *launched* a search boat.
   a. fired
   b. purchased
   c. sent off

6. The shark may have had more deadly *intentions*.
   a. ideas
   b. fins
   c. bites

7. The raft traveled an *incredible* amount in a short time.
   a. wonderful
   b. unbelievable
   c. frightening

Inference

8. What could have been one of the things that drew the sharks' attention toward the raft?
   a. the bright sunshine
   b. the high waves
   c. the girls' splashing

Drawing Conclusions

9. Do you think that officials in the area around the girls' hotel were well prepared for sea rescues?
   a. No, they knew nothing about the raft.
   b. Yes, they sent a plane, boat, and helicopter to help.
   c. Yes, they kept count of all the sharks in the area.

Following Through

10. Look up the United States Coast Guard in an encyclopedia or other reference. Write a paragraph on the services performed by members of the Coast Guard.

MP3391

Junior Ski Patrol

Any skier who has ever had a problem on a snowy mountain knows how important a ski patrol can be. The patrol helps people who fall and are hurt. A skier could lie with a twisted ankle for some time if the ski patrol were not watching. In many ski areas, the National Ski Patrol is looking for young people, from fifteen to eighteen years old, to join the Junior Ski Patrol.

Most of the Junior Ski Patrol members have been skiing since they could walk, but it is not easy to join the patrol. Members must pass tests in first aid, use of a rescue sled, and general skiing.

After students have passed all three tests, they begin work. Their first ski run of the day is a check for possible dangers on the trails. They might find a thin patch of snow or large stones. These spots are then marked so skiers will stay away from them. During the day, the patrol moves up and down the slopes. They are always watching for hurt or tired skiers. In very cold weather, they also look for skiers with signs of frostbite. Frostbite occurs when a part of the body begins to freeze. The patrol can warn freezing skiers to get inside and warm up. They may save a skier from a painful case of frostbite.

The last check run of the day is also very important. Patrollers cover every bit of each slope. They want to be sure no one is left overnight on the trails. Some days are long and difficult for the patrol. But when they can help injured people or keep someone from getting frostbite, they feel like heroes. They even forget their sore muscles and cold feet. The Junior Ski Patrol is a welcome sight on any mountain.

Main Idea

1. This story is mainly about
   a. the dangers of frostbite.
   b. teenage rescue skiers.
   c. first aid stations.

Significant Details

2. On the first run of the day, a junior patroller
   a. looks for hurt skiers.
   b. checks for possible dangers.
   c. makes a trail for skiers.

3. The right age for a junior patroller is
   a. 12 to 15.
   b. 15 to 18.
   c. 18 to 21.

4. The last run of the day is important to the patrol because they
   a. check snow conditions for the next day.
   b. ski with other patrollers.
   c. make certain no one is left overnight.

Inference

5. A patrol member probably learns how to
   a. move a skier who is hurt.
   b. win a ski contest.
   c. ride on a sled.

Drawing Conclusions

6. Anyone who tries out for the Junior Ski Patrol probably
   a. needs a job badly.
   b. is already a very good skier.
   c. will have to leave Colorado.

MP3391

Reversing Falls

Waterfalls are some of nature's most beautiful and useful gifts to the land. They are caused by a sudden and steep drop in a river. For years, people in many countries have depended on waterfalls as power for electricity. As the water falls to a lower level, it can be used to make hydroelectric power.

Waterfalls also give us some breath-taking sights. People travel many miles to see Niagara Falls, one of the wonders of North America. People who visit Victoria Falls in Africa find them to be just as beautiful. Many people go to Venezuela to see the

Angel Falls. With a drop of 3212 feet, Angel Falls is one of the highest waterfalls in the world.

A waterfall in New Brunswick, Canada, causes visitors to stop and stare. It is called the Reversing Falls of St. John and it lives up to its name. Usually water flows along the St. John River and then drops down through a gorge to the Bay of Fundy below. But during high tide the waterfall actually goes in reverse. Water from the bay rushes up the waterfall. People have a hard time believing their eyes. Waterfalls are not supposed to flow upwards.

Actually, there is a simple explanation. When the tide comes in, the water in the Bay of Fundy rises at least five feet higher than the St. John River. Sometimes the water rises as much as ten feet in one hour. As the water in the bay rises, it is pushed up through the gorge. This causes the waterfall to run in reverse.

Main Idea
1. The most unusual waterfall is
   a. Niagara Falls.
   b. Angel Falls.
   c. Reversing Falls.

Significant Details
2. One of the highest waterfalls is in
   a. Venezuela.
   b. Canada.
   c. Africa.
3. Waterfalls can be used for
   a. swimming and recreation.
   b. hydroelectricity.
   c. landmarks.
4. Water usually flows from the St. John River to the Bay of
   a. Victoria.
   b. Fundy.
   c. New Brunswick.

Context Clues
5. A waterfall in New Brunswick goes in *reverse.*
   a. flows in the correct way
   b. flows upwards
   c. increases in size

Inference
6. Would you say that people are impressed with sights of nature?
   a. No, man-made products are more enjoyable.
   b. Yes, many people plan trips around such sights.
   c. No, such things can be very boring.

Drawing Conclusions
7. Would it be better to visit the Falls of St. John after the tide has come in?
   a. Yes, you could get a better view.
   b. No, it would be too dangerous.
   c. Yes, then the Falls reverse.

Supernova—The Exploding Star

It all happened years ago—170,000 years ago to be exact. While early man was just beginning to move around the earth, a star blew up in the sky. It sent out very bright light, traveling at 186,282 miles per second. It was not until February 23, 1987, that the first rays of this light were seen on earth. Ian K. Shelton is a Canadian astronomer. He was looking through a telescope in northern Chili when he saw a very bright star. Shelton had discovered a supernova!

The word *supernova* means "super new star." When a supernova takes place, however, it is really a very old star blowing up and dying. Such stars may be millions of years old.

The supernova seen by Shelton was named 1987A because it was the first supernova of the year. Scientists around the world were excited. NASA scientists quickly pointed their spacecraft and instruments toward the supernova. Voyager 2 had been on its way to Neptune. It turned toward the exploding star. Japan, Australia, Italy, and the Soviet Union turned their instruments, too. They looked toward the Large Magellanic Cloud. This is a small star galaxy of the Milky Way. Supernova 1987A is located in this galaxy. Scientists were very eager to find out all they could about this star. It was the first supernova seen in over 383 years. At last, scientists could study a supernova to try to discover how stars and planets are formed. With new information, they might also be able to predict how long the universe will last.

There are two kinds of supernovae. A star spends most of its time converting hydrogen to helium. After millions of years, the hydrogen in the center of a star burns. Gravity pulls burning gases and other matter to the center of the star. Then the star blows up. This is a Type I supernova. Type II takes place when a star's weight is eight times greater than the sun's. This kind of star is known as a red giant and has its hydrogen around its outer layers. Eventually, the weight of the star can cave in the center. Shock

continued . . .

MP3391

waves are sent to the outer layers of hydrogen causing a huge explosion. A small star is usually left behind. Dust and gases that are scattered throughout the air go on to form new stars and planets.

Supernova 1987A is unusual. Most scientists think it is a Type II supernova. Some, however, think that it could be a Type I. After its bright outer shell of light dies down a little, scientists will be able to answer questions about supernova 1987A and the universe.

Main Idea

1. The term "1987A" refers to
   a. the year the first supernova was discovered.
   b. the supernova that has been found in the Large Magellanic Cloud.
   c. the number of every supernova seen so far.

Significant Details

2. Who discovered 1987A?
   a. NASA scientists
   b. The Voyager 2
   c. Ian K. Shelton

3. Shelton's supernova first blew up
   a. 383 years ago.
   b. 170,000 years ago.
   c. in 1987.

4. Type I supernova occurs when
   a. burning gases go to the center of a star and it blows up.
   b. the center of a star caves in.
   c. a star hits a planet.

5. New stars and planets are formed by
   a. hydrogen.
   b. gravity.
   c. dust and gases.

Context Clues

6. Scientists can *predict* how long the universe will last.
   a. argue
   b. tell what will happen
   c. agree

7. A star spends most of its time *converting* hydrogen to helium.
   a. colliding
   b. changing
   c. collapsing

Drawing Conclusions

8. Why are supernovae so important in scientific study?
   a. They can tell about the life cycles of planets.
   b. They tell the amount of hydrogen in the atmosphere.
   c. There are not many supernovae for scientists to observe.